Chasing a Butterfly

The day is young,
I am strong,
I shall prevail.

—H. W. Bryce

Chasing a Butterfly

H. W. Bryce

*A journey of love
through loss to
acceptance*

Suite 300 - 990 Fort St
Victoria, BC, V8V 3K2
Canada

www.friesenpress.com

ISBN
978-1-4602-9933-3 (Hardcover)
978-1-4602-9934-0 (Paperback)
978-1-4602-9935-7 (eBook)

1. POETRY

Distributed to the trade by The Ingram Book Company

To my Ann, of course,
with my every bit of love.
Thanks for being here.

Acknowledgements

The poems She's Lost, It's A Long, Long Goodbye, Just a Little Girl, and What I Really Wish For first appeared in the 2012 Spring Poetry Anthology Latitude on 2nd.

The Poem Season of Disconnect first appeared as a finalist in the contest winners' anthology, 2012 Summer Poetry Anthology, Latitude on 2nd.

Both publications were by Cool Waters Media, Inc., via its subsidiary Empirical Magazine, in Chico, California, U.S.A.

I am deeply indebted to my wife Ann, of course. Without her suffering, I would never have written these poems. So bittersweet. Forever love.

I owe Dorothy Leclair of the Alzheimer's Society of British Columbia a deep debt of gratitude for her cosmic work in teaching the Alzheimer's Education course, and for her stellar leadership of our Alzheimer's support group. Her personal support and encouragement—invaluable.

I also owe The Support Group many, many thanks for holding me up in the beginning and for their love ever since. Many of my poems were generated by the suffering of my fellow care givers.

In addition, the wonderfully talented poets at Holy Wow Poets in Maple Ridge have been most supportive and helpful.

My special thanks to Candice James, Poet Laureate Emerita, New Westminster, B.C., and to fellow care givers from London, Australia, and the U.S.A., for their kind words of approbation as seen on the back cover of this book. I am deeply indebted to them for their good opinion.

I have chosen to use Canadian spelling throughout.

Table of Contents

Introduction

When I was driven to taking an introductory course to educate myself about my wife's Alzheimer's disease, I became tongue-tied and overwhelmed with emotion. It was then that I found a way to express my grief–by writing my feelings and experiences, in poetry. Over the next couple of years, I had compiled about a hundred poems, longish ones, short ones, haiku-style ones.

We went through the whole Respite support, the final realization that I had to take care of me to be able to take care of her, and eventually the long-term care home stage.

I joined a support group, where I found a home among equals: all were going through the same sort of struggles. The group embraced my poetry. They could relate. So could people at large who do not have Alzheimer's in their family.

We, Ann and I and family, went through the stages of anger, grief, sorrow–all the way to acceptance and back to grief, the entire gamut of loss and the whole grieving process again.

I am forever indebted to the Alzheimer's Society, its education and other programmes, and in particular to our local educator and support group facilitator, Dorothy Leclair.

Partial proceeds from the sale of this book are earmarked for the Alzheimer's Society to help combat this terrible disease.

—

I have broken the poems into groups, loosely following the three main stages of Alzheimer's. I say loosely because the progress along the Alzheimer's journey is quite loose itself, and different in different ways for each "victim" and for each Care Giver and for each family. So my divisions are somewhat arbitrary.

But we get through it. We are stronger than we think.

I write for the people.

I. The Way She Was

She hosted a party, her friends asked me to come;
I was ever so nervous but they said don't be dumb.
But they made us get up and dance in the dark—
Electricity flowed and we both felt a spark,
And we both of us turned and we both of us ran—
I taunted a "catch me if you think that you can."

But then she asked me for dinner at home in her flat,
So I computed to see what time would be that?
But culture in England has the quirkiest notions:
For dinner for her is supper for me
And supper for me must be time for her tea,
As she does the brekky, the lunch and the dinner and tea
And I do the breakfast and dinner and sup, don't you see?
Not to mention elevenses or brunches or afternoon
munches—
So I calculated, translated, guaranteed a good fate—
But when I arrived for her dinner, I was four hours too late.

Now lateness for her is a passionate hate,
So when I arrived on her step for that very first date,
She scolded me, harsh!...then invited me in,
And I had to atone for committing that sin;
So I ate in discomfort, the hour was long—
I guess I computed the time a bit wrong.

But though she was angry, all was not lost,
She mellowed right out and I never felt bossed—
But always I wonder if she'd slammed that front door,
Or what if I'd turned and cowardly fled?
We'd never have wed and shared the same bed;
I'm ever so glad that I stayed for that dinner instead.

TALK! TALK! TALK!

Talk! Talk! Talk! Oh, that gift of talk!
How that woman could talk, talk, talk.
She could talk of this, talk of that—
Talk you beneath the talk, talk mat!

Philosophic talk—easy do.
Prove, disprove a point, false or true,
She'd talk with you, she'd talk with pros,
She'd talk with anyone who knows.

Politics? She would claim the realm.
She'd talk, talk, talk, remaining calm,
This side, that side, she'd take a stand,
She always had a but or and.

Religion, too, she'd choose a course,
Run an argue, use fierceful force.
She'd stay the course and wear you down,
But never make you feel a clown.

Admit defeat? Not in her blood,
She'd argue, argue, chew the cud,
And talk and talk, till cows came home—
So who knows what's inside her dome?

Gossip? She'd share like anyone
And go away as if she'd won,
And talk to all, the high, the low,
And never deal a lowly blow.
But people heard and paid her heed,
She knew just how to meet their need.
She'd talk to you, she'd talk to me—
Any excuse to talk, you see.

How she did it I'll never know,
But her pearls of wisdom I duly stow.
Besides all that, come high and low,
She was the smartest talker I'll ever know!

———————————

Bullies, hatred, slam
Swearing, fighting, putting down
Dignity beats all

THE FORSYTHIA SAGA

My lady from England met a lady from there
as we city folk moved to a leftover farm,
and my lady she'd fallen in love with a bush,
and the lady from there said, "Forsythia!" with a hush.

My lady from England tried to cut off a branch
while using a buttering knife,
so I cut some for her and she trimmed them to plant
outside of the place where she cooked.

Well the forsythia thrived and the forsythia bloomed
and it seemed like Time itself had zoomed,
and life in the country was a living Wow!
Until we met Sarah the cow!

It happened when the lady from there
said she had to go away for a while
but that Sarah, her cow, had to stay,
and for her keep, her milk would be pay.

Well my lady from England of course volunteered
and we boys had to milk, though our eyes over-teared,
and my lady's homemade butter sat and went stale,
though the forsythia tree blossomed a gale.

Until came the day through the window she looked
with pride and a smile on her forsythia bush,
and saw Sarah the cow with her tongue curled around
and stripping each leaf; my lady was really dumfound.
Well that was an omen of impending doom,
And my lady screamed and we all gave chase
to corral that cow back to her home base.
But Sarah the cow was winning the race.

Sarah was dragging her tethering rope,
and we all ran like crazy to catch hold of it,
but Sarah the cow turned and mooed right at us,
then turned and took off like a bus.

An almighty chase then ensued
and the family scrambled to capture that cow,
but the closer we got, the harder she'd run
and she scattered us like we were nothing but scum.

She charged at us each, one at a time,
and we had to scramble away from her horns
and each time we thought we'd got her, she'd balk,
and we had to regroup and re-stalk.

We got her surrounded and she mooed like a moose
and as we got closer, once again she broke loose,
until our first born got a hold of the rope
and we tied her up to the van.

Then I drove the van right back to the farm
with Sarah dragging me back like a ton
and the family pushing her on at the back,
and we dragged her back off to the barn.

Then we went back to that Forsythia bush,
where it stood all bedraggled and sad,
and so to her most beloved forsythia,
my lady had to bid a sad sayonaria.

But the next batch of butter worked out,
for my lady had learned that it first had to hang to drip-dry.
Sadly the lesson from this my lady never did learn,
for the next volunteer were those wretch wee pups.

THE QUEEN OF THE BALL

When I met the lady
She was in her prime,
She was vivid, alive and living with style,
She gave any place
Its warm pleasant clime,
And nobody else
Could match her sweet smile.

She bedazzled the crowd
When she entered the room,
She was sexy and had that come-hither stare;
She took over the room
Like a shining new moon,
Ever mysterious,
She was a force in full bloom.

She was a wow with the boys and the girls,
Her birthday parties
Were a must for the moms,
She could play the kids' games
And talk with the moms as one of the girls
Of business, or hearsay, religion,
Or fashion or curls.

She could run a committee
So smooth she could soothe
The savagest breast and
Find compromise.
She could talk to mayors as well as street folk,
Yet she could appreciate most any old joke.

And for any cause, she could raise a ton,
She'd marathon till her legs gave out,
Once she got started

There was no stopping her,
She'd give it her all
And hold back nothing at all.

Business or pleasure
She always spoke well,
She'd never betray
A trade secret or private detail,
Never would slander or tell a lie,
And never did poke
Anyone's figurative eye.

And through it all
She was the picture of grace.
She always gave people
The space they needed to serve,
Always encouraged each person's dreams
And gave them the dignity
That we all deserve

There was no doubt the lady had style,
She gave out no secrets, enthralled us all,
She never gave in to unseemly bile;
She was the obvious queen of the ball.

WINE AND CHEESE DAYS

I remember all our wine and cheese days,
Warm gatherings saved up for for months;
I remember how you chose the cheese,
How carefully you matched them with the wines.
I recall warm talk and aging friendships,
How you were the hostess with the most,
And I was there to raise the toast.

How I loved the view of life we had then,
There was never any strife then,
Every morn was fresh and new then,
In our days of wine and cheese.
We kept too busy to be dour then,
How rich we were then, though poor.

I always said, it was our prayer,
My silly toast thrown up from our cozy lair:
May we age like wine and keep like cheese,
May our lives always be a breeze,
May all our days be wine and cheese,
And may our hearts never ever freeze.

So here's to wine and cheese, dear,
Here's to that loving squeeze, dear,
I thank you for your loving ways, dear,
I cherish all the days we spent as one,
Never was there any better
Than our heady wine and cheese days.

We were matched like fine cheese and wine,
Paired for life, set to dine on love alone.

A loaf of homemade bread,
A glass of wine and you dear,
What more could a fellow want?

II. Early Stages, Early Warnings

I, Vispilio, have come to conquer!
Be prepared to bow before me
And kneel devoutly before my altar.
Wait no longer for him, for I am he!

I, Vispilio, am called Thief by Night.
Men of great knowledge have dubbed me thus,
Though I have many names--Latrunculus,
Il Ladro, Il Fus, Raptor, Eremptor:
Thief, ravisher, robber—I have my will—
As a thief by any name is still a thief,
Therefore, I, Vispilio, am called The Thief.

I come from a proud tradition, indeed,
For it is well known that lawyers are thieves,
And politicians, who lie to you
And do the opposite, but tax you ever.
And businessmen are thieves, as well you know,
For they falsify their costs and magnify
Their profits, all at your expense.

Yet these are honourable men
Who have the respect of society.
And so I, Vispilio, Master Thief,
Do have the respect and the honour among thieves.

So beware, and prepare, for I, Vispilio,
Am coming for you, and I shall have you.
I shall crack the safe that is your cranium
And I shall crawl the channels of your brain.
I shall collect the power in your synapses,
For that is the manna that makes me strong,

I shall gather up all your memories
And take off with your feeble skills;
I'll burgle your dendrites and uncross your tees,
I'll scramble your axons and leave you in spills.

And I'll bundle the lot in my burgalar's bag
And—fear not, for I never bungle a job—
I'll leave you intact—except for all that—
For thievery is an honourable job.

So I'm coming to get you, you cannot resist,
I serve my master well, and, like he,
I come by stealth to build my wealth,
And no man of science can stop me—
For even mighty he have I robbed!

So prepare yourself to meet your master.
You cannot fight and win, for I am strong;
Whatever you do, I'll show you wrong.
Heed he who speaks, it is I, Vispilio!

———————

Adversity wins
Man stiffens his back
The spirit of strength

Feelin' kinda frail,
Lookin' kinda pale
Must be time to bail
    Escape this gloomy mood

Must be feelin' age
Could be just a stage
Tryin' not to rage
    Time to change this mood

Legs are feelin' wobbly
Toes are feelin' bobbly
Movement kinda hobbly
    Outpaced now by the brood

Hands are feelin' clumsy
Eyes are feelin' wumsy
Gut is lookin' dumpsy
    Damn this lousy mood

Feelin' kinda peaky
Brain is feelin' leaky
Body's feelin' creeky
    Coulda been the food

Feelin' kinda owly
Face is lookin' jowly
Tum is feelin' bowely
    Still I mustn't brood

Feelin' kinda frail
Lookin' kinda pale
Must be time to bail
    Escape this gloomy mood

Been sittin' as a giver
It's hard upon the liver
Life is like a river
      Ever changing mood

What the heck to do
Nothin' seems like new
Didn't pay to be a shrew
      Life it seems I blew

Guess I'll turn a leaf
Turn away the grief
Find that big relief
      Find that happy mood

Then I'll feel so groovy
And never again so boozy
And life again'll be a doozy
      Now this I call a mood

Life's too good to bail
Grass is green this side of pale
No longer feelin' frail
      Can't help this happy mood

(This poem was written early on along the Memory Loss Road. I was seeing changes in Ann but was reluctant to accept them as symptoms. I tried to express my feelings as they bounced off Ann's. I was also trying to keep my spirits up.)

Old age is just a state of mind
It's only what you make of it
If along the way you can be kind
Then you'll be fine at the end of it

Middle age is just a state of mind
A balance of your work and rest
A chase to not be left behind
Or a chance to be your very best

Youth is a just state of mind
It's either waste or epic blast
You can be the orange or you can be the rind
It all depends on how you let yourself be cast

And Oh! To be a babe again!
To be loved for what I am
And not for what I could or should become
But just for being what I am

(Here Ann was showing signs of unfamiliar behaviour, such as asking the same question over and over. Our daughter-in-law suggested we attend the Over Fifties group. We did, and I found myself starting to express myself in poetry. This one was a fight against growing old, and against these new behaviours.)

Also it expresses the regression in the mind of the Alzheimer's person.

WHERE ARE YOU, LOVE

Where are you, love?
Where have you gone?
Have you gone a-wandering again?
To what historic spot?
To where you were when you were young?
Or to some enchanted place?
Are you? Or are you not
...Pixilated now?

Have you gone in haste?
Have you time to waste?
Is there time to taste
The wine with honey laced?

Come back, my love,
Come back to me.
I miss your quaintly charm.
I miss the laughs,
I miss the gaffs,
I miss your baking flops;
I even love that you're half barm.
I hope you never come to harm!

Are you lost, my love?
Can you call?
Can I come to you?
Where are you, love?
Where is it that you've gone?
I miss you much,
Your touch, and such,
Are you gone for long?
How can I keep in touch?

I see you there but where, oh where
Is it that your mind has gone?
Have I lost my touch?
Do I mean so much
That I captivate you not?
What have I done?
Or is it something else?
Speak to me, I die to know,
Can you still give love?

Where are you love,
Where have you gone?
I'm trying to be strong.
I am here, I'm always here.
I'll wait for you, I'll wait on you,
I'll be forever here and true.
If you're here, or if you're there,
I know you're always you.

I know, inside, you're you.

Hello? It's me.
Do you know me, love?

Now I am admitting to seeing behaviours as symptoms. But what to do
with that? This was one of my early attempts. I read this next poem,
"Sometimes," to an Over Fifties group. Some thought I'd taken it from a
book. The leader wanted it for the group's theme.

SOMETIMES

Sometimes the world will fail us.
Sometimes people do.
Sometimes we fail our selves.
Sometimes our lives just fall apart.

In those sometime moments,
The sometimes when words do fail...
Sometimes a hug will help.
A kiss upon the cheek,
A holding of the hands,
To hold us in one piece.

In these, our sometime moments,
Or when, in the face of tragedy,
When no comedy will do,
When our stock of words runs dry
And we hurt so hard we can't so much as cry,
Sometimes, a hug will help.

I know it's cliché to say,
But even pain is temporary.
So don't let the bastards make you worry,
Make your grief to tell a better story.

And give a hug a day, kiss a needy cheek,
Hold out a friendly hand, take that nobler stand
In spite of inclement Sometimes,
Help hold a friend together.
Sometimes a hug will help.

She's in there, somewhere, she is!
She's fighting to get out, I know.
You think you see her—see?
But when you look, she only seems to be.

Look again. You can see her, through her eyes,
Plaintive, pleading. In there, there's no disguise.
You can see that she was wise—
You can see the person, in there. See?

But out here, she seems to be,
To you who do not know her,
Something of a fool,
For her words are not words,
Her thoughts are not thoughts—
Not to our ears, as her sentences—
They're never quite finished.

But inside, she still knows,
And she still lives, in there, alone,
Inside herself, she is.
She is.

RE She's In There: Story on CBC TV Nov 13, 2012: Doctors communicate with a man in a vegetative state: Mr. Routley, London U: He responds to questions, as in, he indicates that: I am not in pain. i.e., his brain is very active. So I wrote: I'm right, Ann is in there, her brain is still alive, and she understands just about everything that's said; she just can't speak or react as before.

JENNIFER

She kneels before us
And bathes our feet.
Gently she towels them down
And trims our nails.
With humble love she serves us
And gives us, with respect
Which we probably have not earned,
Tender affirmation.
She is a care giver.
But not just a giver of care,
A giver of kindness,
Unsolicited but not unwanted,
A glowing example of a gifted soul,
A blessing, heart to heart.
The silent pleasure we feel
Escapes in a grateful sigh.
We part in the warmth of hugs,
And a promise to spread the care.
Jennifer.

Native to the few
Foreign to the many
Dignity

Those shoes! Those shoes!
Those wretched shoes of hers.
I swear they walk, all on their own.
Upon my soul, it makes me groan.

Preparing for a shopping trip,
It took an hour to find a matching pair of shoes.
"I left them for you, in standard pairs,
I left them in a neat array upon that old book case,
The one you'd shed of books,
I left them on the bottom shelf."
She wandered down the hall to see,
And groaned as if she were in pain—
And then came back with a picture frame.

I huffed impatient and went myself,
Only to find the shelves in disarray.
One white shoe, one brown, two loafers of different styles.
No matching pair. No two alike.
Some of them must be on a hike.
All of this, of course, to my dismay.

She chose a black loafer style to wear
And then it was a tear to find a match to make a pair.
I hunted here and I hunted there,
The match was neither here nor there.
I hunted hither, I hunted thither,
I got myself in such a dither!

Well, when a thing ain't where it ought to be,
You look in places where it oughn't ought to be.
I found the missing shoe...inside our bed,
Down at the foot, between the sheets.

When at last her feet were shod—
She didn't want to go!
I checked the clock and sure enough
It was too late.
The shops in town were closed.

So I re-arranged her shoes,
I mean ALL her shoes!
(For the umptieth time I think.)
Upon that old bookcase—
The one she'd shed of books—
And parked the neat black loafers
Beside her chair, ready for a tearing start next day.

Next day, while dressing to go out,
(Getting ready was such a bout)
It came the time to don her shoes.
But her shoes, as if by magic, were no longer there.
I shouldn't say, but I dare:
Her shoes apparently had walked,
(I shouldn't wonder if they talked)
In the middle of the night.
It gave us such a fright.
And so those shoes I stalked;
I gave search and hunted with all my might.

With might, though, might not be right.
For they managed to elude my sight.
For those shoes, those wretched shoes,
Were on the prowl again.

Three separate shoes were in the living room,
(The start of a footwear boom?)
And one stray shoe sat beside the exit door.

And one lone sabot was kissing the hallway floor.
Three unrelated shoes were in the kitchen (by the stove)...
And I swear I saw a bootie in the garden grove.

How they all got there is a wonderment to me;
They seem to hop like a circus jumping flea.
Oh 'tis a worrisome thing to see
How a shoe can get the betterment of me.
Oh woe! Alack! Alas! And moan!
How a shoe can walk all on its own!

For I found the missing loafer...in the veggie bin.
(What it was doing there may well have been a sin.)
Too late to make our appointment now,
I shook my head and uttered one bewildered, "Wow!"

And when I knelt to put them on,
She didn't want to put her footie in.
And I swear I saw a cheeky grin—
I'm sure she saw the humour there within.

Next day, we tried it once again,
Although, for sure, it was in vain.

She wanted to wear her brand new runner.
The game became a bummer.
I said, "They're not so a propos."
Her scowl conveyed an undertow!

"Fine," I said, "try on your old sabot."
Her curt reply was simply, "No!"
I then suggested she wear a loafer,
"Yuck!" she gasped, "nothing could be grosser."

And in the end we chose a pump,
Although she still nicknamed me a Grump,
And finally when all was done, and we began the walking on,
The reason that we had for that...
Well it was lost and it was gone!

Those shoes! Those shoes! Back in a clump.
Half should go to the city dump.
But how to find the missing ones, you see,
Needs must have so many clues.
Save me Lord. Those shoes! Those shoes!

Then once again, my friend, to get those shoes,
I must admit, I had the blues.
I swear those shoes, they do the opposite of spawn,
For half her shoes again were up and gone!

Who said those shoes were made for walking?
Now it's me to whom I'm talking!
Metaphorically they've walked all over me.
To whom to turn to cancel their decree
And make them stop me talking back to me?

I guess I'll have to do the shopping all alone
And have someone sit beside those shoes—
I mean with her, she needs a break from me;
I'm not sure just which of us has lost our sanity.

So please, no more talk of shoes.
Those shoes! Those shoes!
They'll be the death of me!
I'll have to take a cruise
And search each Seven Sea
And hope to find my lost and former sanity.

MEMORABILIA

Oh dear!
A little pile of business cards,
An empty CD box,
Picture postcards—an owl, a heron, one red fox,
An orange, a thumb tack, and one stopped watch,
All sitting on the stand under the kitchen light,
Balanced beside one lady's slipper, the right.
Ann was here!

———————————

In weakness or strength
In peace or in war
Human condition

Hope is eternal, or that's what they say.
They say give up on your hope and you'll die.
They also say that salvation's at hand
In that moment you give up on your hope.
Don't you believe that hope is so fickle,
Do and your strength will slow to a trickle;
You have to believe for things to work out.
And let me say this, that hope's the real deal
And don't let anyone steal that from you,
For hope will encourage and lend you the strength
To fight the good fight and to see some light
At the end of your journey's dark tunnel,
'Cause if you give up, you're Misery's delight
And each corner will give you a new fright.

Respect for others.
Respect for self.
Common Sense.

III. Middle Stages

She's lost all her nouns, she's misplaced them all.
We've searched for them, for she talks with a scrawl,
But names are all blank and things are hand signs,
Then it all proves futile and we end up with sighs.

She's lost all her verbs, we've looked everywhere.
We've checked all the books but her verbs aren't there.
We've looked in drawers, we've looked on shelves,
We've even looked inside ourselves.

We ask her what she means and she tries to tell.
She searches her brain, she tries to spell.
She knows it's all in there—it's sealed in a box,
But she has no key and her tongue trips as she talks.

She's lost her directions, she knows not where;
When she should turn left, she stops with a stare.
She looks all around the compass and all,
But she cannot find those directions at all.

And instructions misguide her, when given a task
She'll bring you a towel when a dish was the ask.
Recipes confuse and it all goes in one pot,
And for low on the stove, she will turn it to hot.

She's lost all our faces, they're not in her purse,
Instead of a memory, things are a curse.
Instead of her mate, she thinks I'm her brother,
In place of herself, she's become someone other.

She keeps on looking for the pieces she's lost,
It's terrible to see such a terrible cost,
To see such a life so terribly tossed.
Alas, it is true, that truly she's lost!

I wish I were that young again,
She'd said one day in reminiscing,
And as she watched the children play,
I sensed a change in her that day.

That was many years gone by,
And life for her is passing by;
Her oldest memories keep coming back,
Until today's are blurred or blank.

For nostalgia's happy days are catching,
And she tries to do the things she did back then,
In her childhood days, in her childhood ways,
Each tiff, each cry, each helpful giving way replays.

And now as life goes day by day
And life is hard to be enduring,
Her thoughts and speech in disarray,
She's even forgotten how to play.

And now she's just a little girl again,
It's there her mind is dwelling,
She does the things she did back then
So now I know the girl she was back when.

Yes, she is that little girl again,
But she's gifted me the memories,
And these true treasures do I keep,
To dream again upon my sleep.

Yes, dear, the memories will stay with me,
For life with you has been a spree;
And thanks, my love, for everything,
I wouldn't trade for anything.
I wouldn't trade the little girl,

Nor trade the lady then,
Nor would I be without our life
That you give me still, my darling wife.

For now I am the richer man
For having shared a life with her.
Now all the love she gave to me, so true,
I gladly share with you.

———————————

Good deeds and honour
Together like arms and hugs
Trust the Madonna

DIGNITY IS THE DARNEDEST OF THINGS!

Dignity is the darnedest of things!
It needs to be free to spread its wings.
It's free to be had if you have the will,
If you're wanting in pride it fits the bill.

Some say it's ours as a right for all of Man,
That it's the centre of a vast eternal plan
But make no mistake, we'll have to fight
To earn our dignity and wear its light.

Dignity comes through examples of good,
It's how we would be if only we could.
So let us now set our dignity free,
Let our own true Self be our own true Me.

For it's the caring and sharing and even the daring,
The support and rapport that dignity brings;
We do it for others to help heal their stings,
It's the centre of life, it's why our soul sings.

It survives oppression, depression and war,
It soothes a sore heart and eases life's scar,
It bolsters the most modest of modesty's prides,
And cushions the bumps on life's roughest of rides.

Dignity comes through examples of good,
It's how we would be if only we could.
So let us now set our dignity free,
Let our own true Self be our own true Me.

Yes dignity is the darnedest thing!
Dignity is the best kind of bling.
It's the courage and pride that dignity brings,
It's the centre of life, it's why our soul sings.

She'll drive you crazy making you wait getting ready,
Then changes her mind and changes her clothes.
You wonder inside if her mind's set on close.
She expects you, of course, to also be ready.
The challenge of course is to keep yourself steady.
When she's all dressed up an hour before—
And the event doesn't start for three hours or more—
She'll steam at the ears and you'll suffer your fears
The whole ride to there, and she may shed a few tears,
Then berate you for wasting so much time at the hall,
Until the people show up, then she'll snap a new mood
And greet the good folk with her good attitude;
And you'll feel once again you've been royally screwed.

Oh she can seem to be rude, and appear so unkind,
And it's not easy to cope or a thumb rule to find,
But it's not the Female that's in her so much as Disease,
It removes the Adult and implants the Child inside;
And you, poor male, cannot win against this new tide.
So what the norm was between you no longer holds sway,
You have to learn some new dances to keep out of her way,
And that ain't easy, for patience like this will need a new art,
If you don't have it by nature, you have to be taught;
You have to rehearse, make ad lib a centrifugal part,
And practise and practise, it cannot be bought.
So work on your patience, work on your skills,
It's no longer the classic old battle of wills,
It's a new game of challenge not the old one of teasy,
For sure learning such patience is certainly not easy.

What I really, really wish for
Is an end to all Dementia,
For Alzheimer and his lie
To permanently die.

Gladly I would be assassin
And take that sweet revenge,
And those who struggle to survive
Would know that they're alive.

I gladly would attend his funeral
And heap his grave with weeds.
I'd make his memory so marginal
It would cut off his "in" to all.

But for all the lives he's taken,
And all the grief he's left,
I'd force him to atone this bane
And make him take away the pain.

I'd make him tell us why such pain,
What source had wrought such evil.
I'd make sure he never did again
Such acts that are Medieval.

So what I really wish for
Is suffering's demise,
For people not to have to cry,
For Alzheimer now to die!

But most of all I'd ban the one
Alzheimer's brutal thievery
That would steal a person's only mind,
And save us each from all his kind.

You cannot argue with the Alzheimer,
We don't know where he's from,
We don't know where he goes,
We don't know where he gets his strength,
His ins and outs or breadth and length;
But we know he robs his victims
Of their means to think and talk,
And in the end, the very skill to walk.

So it takes a deal of patience
To deal with one who suffers this disease;
To think that they are stupid is a myth,
For something in them still is sparking
And they will plug away determined
To have their will and go their way.

For they are used to living as their own
And it's hard to let that go and to accept "forget,"
And though it's cruel and never fair,
You have to help them live the life that's in them yet.

Oh, you can try to argue
Because you know that you are right,
But to argue is to pick a fight,
And you know you'll never dim their light.

So if they think they're going back
To London, Prague, or France,
It's not for us to plead and prance,
But to assure them all is well,
That you can enjoy each other for a spell,
For now they're safe, and that you've got their back.

Change the subject, change the task,
Chances are they'll forget to ask
Again for quite a while.
Then choose a happy style
And try to fill the holes
That now fill mem'ry's roles.

Yes you can try to argue
Because you know that you are right;
But this will leave you in frustration,
With no means for restoration,
For your logic is never going to cut it,
Where there is no logic to be had.

No, you cannot argue with the Alzheimer's,
It's as dense as a sack of ball-peen hammers;
Though the victims held within its grip
Are innocent, their needs repeat and stick.
So when they ask a task you cannot grant,
The best approach is to be frank,
Like the wise old Monk up in the Abbey:
You can be right, or you can be happy!

If wishes were trees
And each tree were a forest
Each day would give us a feast

This is the season of her disconnect,
Made inglorious by this wretched Thief
Who brought such clouds that lour upon her brow
And lie now deep within her bosom.

And now is my brow wreathed in frowns
Of deep confusion and hard, bruise-ed hurt.
Our once merry greetings now stern alarms,
Our delightful dances now dread creepings.
Grim-visag'd Thief of brain our brows do wrinkle
And now, instead of mounting unified front,
She dances for a diff'rent demon,
For the Thief has shrunk her brain,
And laughs lascivious, this evil lout.

For he is not "shap'd for sporting tricks,"
Nor made to court and make us into happy folks,
He that is rudely formed, and wants of love's true majesty.
Yet he struts forth boldly to mis-shape our sense
And remake our thoughts, curtailed, to match his twisted
own;

For the Thief does feel so cheated out of features,
By what it pleases him to call "dissembling nature,"
That obsessed is he to now deform
And leave unfinish-ed and out of rhyme,
This living, breathing poetry,
This love I proudly call my own,
Truncate long before her time.

So resentful and unfashionable has he become
That dogs do bark upon his very shadow.
And yet he laughs, as my love, she whiles away her time
In sorting through her bobbles and in folding of the sheets.

...And in refolding of the sheets...

Now, since he has no delight in the company of self,
Yet plays upon his shadow, even as he shuns the sun,
The while obsessing on his own deformity,
He waxes eloquent he's now diminished her to childhood.

And since he cannot prove himself a lover,
Or entertain us fair well-spoken folk,
He is determined to prove himself the villain.

So, as he's come to hate the bright and beautiful,
He scornful struts success with over stretched pride,
And revelling that now he has destroyed her soul,
He thus does practice villainy to gross excess!

It rankles hard to hear him plotting such "inductions
dangerous"
By stealing into brains and cutting their connections
While he puts an end upon our dreams,
And makes of us the strangers in her eyes
Who once were lovers, sons, and kinfolk.
Then as he is subtle, false, and treacherous,
She now is lost and lonely and confused;
Pathetic now it is to see her thus.
And thus, the Thief has ripped our hearts right out.

But being we of stronger mettle,
And of sane and scientific mind,
We shall mount a counter battle
Such the Thief has never seen,
And with a whirlwind siege we'll wind
Round his fortress where it's never been

That either he'll surrender him,
Or he will burn, forever burn.

And peace shall reign from now.

Amen.

With thanks to King Richard III (and William Shakespeare)

———————

Dignity Alphabet

Doing onto others
Igniting one's worth
Giving freely
Never putting down
Intolerance put to rest
Truth
Yielding to the call of duty

I REMEMBER

I remember the good times
When every season was summer
Because I was with you

I remember excitement
How my pulse coursed so hot
Because I was with you

I remember bad times
And how we survived
Because I was with you

I remember love times
Our forever love times
Because I'm always with you

Memory is short,
Unless you pay attention.
Making legacy.

My loved one is ill, I must go to her
For she is in her hour of need
The call to duty I now must heed
For I have sworn an oath of faith with her

I must heed this call to duty
For it's the honest thing to do
And service is a thing of beauty
Understood but by the few

I must go to her and serve
And put my needs on hold
I must respect that she'll deserve
My most devoted action given bold

I must learn now to give to others
To give up all my childish things
And treat all beings as my brothers
And strive to earn my duty's wings

I must learn from brave examples
Of those who've gone before
I must serve as they have served
Their duties done in days of yore

I am called to duty
It's come my time to serve
I must give my time quite free
For lives may well depend on me

She tried to sit upon the couch
    But Kitty cat was there
She tried to sit her down to eat
    But Kitty cat was there
She took a stroll and tried to think
    But Kitty cat was there
She went from dining room to kitchen sink
And from the sink into her den
    And Kitty cat was there

She worked and then she headed for
Her favourite easy chair
But wouldn't you just know?
Yes you know
    Kitty cat was there
Come end of day and tired out
She tried to go to bed
And bless my soul
Of course, you know
    Kitty cat was there

Should she despair?
Is this a something to repair?
I'm thinking not,
Just pick a spot, and worry not
    Kitty cat will first be there
So she cuddles up with Kitty cat
For you cannot make a cat to scat
For truth be told that in the end
    Kitty cat's your friend

She fills me with such utter wonder,
As does the lightning, rain and thunder.

I do admire her gracious beauty,
The ease with which she does her duty.

I feel the brilliant colours of her inner life,
I sense her vibrant zestful challenge facing strife.

And how it makes me long to fly;
We'd soar like hawks up to the sky.

We'd find some far-off magic bower
And live forever, oh, to have such magic power.

But I can never know the stages of her being,
Or if this scary journey will be freeing.

For I can never feel the wind against her cheeks
As free she flits about the flowers all along the creeks.

And I can never see the sights that she can see
From heights her butterfly keen eyes can see.

Nor can I feel the pain she feels
As when the ruthless net her freedom steals.

And then how hard becomes the effort,
When there's a storm in every port.

And when they "pin her to a card" for show
For students now to learn and then to know

The why, the where, the how and when,
And will true peace for her come then?

And will they solve the mysteries of life
And make a world to end her misery and strife?

How brutally from freedom she's been torn
And wrenched right back to ovum. Again to be reborn?

Then as she goes into her shell to incubate a spell,
The world and I are quite shut out without a word to tell.

But suddenly she shines so caterpillar like,
Alive in colour ready, now to have at life.

But then, Alas! The magic flies away again,
And I am left with yearnings running full a-main

How long will she be living in this chrysalis?
How hard the battle fought? How dark a life like this?

I see her in my mind so fully blossomed
I can't believe her life is in its autumn.

And then like magic she blossoms there in full array!
Oh God I wish you'd let her stay!

Oh how I long to fly beside her butterflying side,
To match her mighty awesome stride,
For her to sprinkle from her wings that magic powder
Over me that I might fly with her into her magic bower

(Sigh)
But I can never know just how to fly
Nor how to BE a butterfly...

And yet...
She fills me with such utter wonder,
As does the lightning, rain, and thunder.

([...it's granting another his/her own self-respect]–to signify that a being
has an innate right to be valued and receive ethical treatment. Wikipedia)

Dignity is...

Facing the slings and the arrows of life's every curve
While standing there firm without losing your nerve;
It's fighting back without stooping to slur,
Without losing control or pretending to purr,
Taking life's beating without stooping to beg,
Or trying to take someone down just a peg;
It's the taking another one's heaviest burden
Without the complaining or sticking a word in,
Or laying a plan to get back with a plot
When someone drops you in a desperate spot;
It's accepting rewards or a gift or a thanks
So the giver will think that he's rich like the banks,
And the same with insults, the sneers or the put-downs
When you give them the smile and dispense with the
frowns...
Do all of that with aplomb as the coolest of cool
And not making the other one feel like a fool—
If you can do that, then it is you who will win,
And dignity's yours, my Gunga friend Din.

...Dignity

When I knew some of the philosophy
But had none of the experience,
I would wax most eloquently;
After all, I had read all about it,
And never had cause to doubt it.

Until I met the actual thing head on
And went directly into shock!
It frightened me, I lost my wit,
It jerked me from my dreamland
And stopped my inner band.

I had to learn to cope—and how to hope,
And learn to listen, for she never spoke,
For she'd been overcome by a malady.
While the art of thinking gives you clues,
Trial and error pays your dues.

So I failed in my philosophy,
I learned a lesson of humility.
Never now do I presume to know
Things I haven't done or won.
Experience trumps Philosophy 101.

———

Dignity
Like a stately tree
Standing tall

It's a long, long goodbye
When the Thief takes your love away;
One day he slips your guard right by
And things begin to change.

Your daily seas from then get rough
And storms beset your nerve.
How can you fight a thief
Who operates by sleight?

What law of nature grants this thief
His mighty, stealthy ways?
How did you miss his furtive steps
And miss her strange new little ways?

If we could wind the clock right back,
Castrate him of his evil ways,
If we could have a second chance
To better live that first unnoticed day...

Ah! But...until we figure all this out,
Know this, Essential You
Is what I love and who I love,
And curse this thieving lout!

But for all of that and all of that,
Throughout these tortured days,
We'll seek and find some working ways
To work through this and that.

And a wee g'bye will I say
Each and every day, I will.
And for every day I will say
I love you, and I always will.

Until the final goodbye drops in on us,
This will be our long goodbye:
A hug, a kiss, and bless this time for us,
Enjoy our long, and long goodbye.

Dignity a gift.
Dignity a right.
Dignity is earned.

They spit upon the poor old man
They robbed him of his things
They even broke his loving cup
Yet he limped away with chin still up

They scorned the poor old lady
They hurt her till she cried
The lady wished that she could die
Yet she walked away with head held high

So the robbers were the poorer men
For things are only things
And honour is the honest hymn
The injured has inside of him

Giving one his dignity
Is like giving blood—
It lifts his spirits up

KILL 'EM ALL

Kill 'em all, kill 'em all,
The cancers, dementias, and all,
Kill all the germs and diseases that wrack,
Kill all bacteria, give microbes a smack.

Let's kill all paralyses, sex'al disease,
Obesity, flu, and diabetes,
Choke everything that makes you to wheeze,
Let's kill 'em all and make life a breeze.

These diseases must go, they do us no good,
They kill everything in your neighbourhood;
They'll ravage your soul and pick at your skin,
They'll savage your brain and leave you so thin.

So come all you doctors, and scientists, too,
Bring your medical tricks and researchers' kung fu.
Let's kill all the germs and diseases that wrack,
Let us now launch a killing attack.

So, kill 'em all, kill 'em all,
Let's all do a victory dance,
Those diseases are dead and that is a fact,
They've all gone to hell and they'll never come back.

So Hallelujah and say your farewell,
Good riddance bad rubbish, now all will be well,
Welcome all patients, we're glad you are back,
Fear not those germs, now they cannot attack.

So...Kill 'em all, kill 'em all,
The cancers, dementias, and all,
Kill all the germs and diseases that wrack,
Kill all bacteria, give microbes a smack!

COURAGE

When adversity calls
(and you don't have the balls)
And the world gets into your face
And your heart increases its pace
And your body screams "time to take flight"
'Cause you're too scared to stand up and fight—
It's time to take hold of your courage!

When the fates are against you and winning
And you are the one taking a skinning
And the tunnel looks black
And you yearn to go back
But the world won't let go
And you know repercussions will flow—
It's time for the birth of your courage!

For your courage will save you from that,
If you fight for the victory hat,
For proof against evil diversity
Is taught in life's big university
And you learn by the practice of valour
And you gain respect and esteem and power—
Yes it's time to call on your courage!

So come on all you timids and hear,
It's no shame to be feeling the fear,
Remember that facing it full
And fighting in spite of its pull
Is exactly the meaning of valour.
Don't let your soul feel it's being discouraged—
Step right up and show the beggars your courage!

NICE LADY

We were in the store for shopping,
Nothing else at all, when,
Upon a whim she dashed aside
To accost the lady stocking shelves.

She babbled on nonsensically
And I feared the lady would feel fear,
But to my surprise and my delight,
The woman stopped to hear.

I tried, but stayed my intervention,
Signalling instead it's time to go;
The lady then surprised me
And hugged and kissed my Her.

My She said thank you, thank you,
And the two held parting hands,
While I held my breath
And fought to stop a tear.

Oh if only there were more like her,
The lady in the store,
To take the time to recognize
Those poor souls whose lives are hurt.

So many thanks give I
For such good and gen'rous souls,
To feel for those who haven't,
From those who have it all.

Dignity is the UN of our traits.
It fights for fairness for all in all ways,
It gives us the strength to stand up to our Fate,
It spreads its respect and defends against hate.

It stands for you and for me in equality,
It aids us in our responsibility,
It supports us ever to perform every duty,
It brings out of us our innermost beauty.

It supports the weak and spirits the meek,
It keeps the peace that all of us seek,
It brings us together as one neighbourhood,
It celebrates every one's personhood.

It's keep our chin up to smile at our foe,
It keeps our deep-seated sense of honour in tow.
It's pride in our fellows, it's giving out praise;
Yes dignity is the UN of our traits

Little old lady passing by
Cane tap-tap-tapping
Hearts aflutter sigh

FRAIL

She stood tall, and she strode strong,
She never put a foot down wrong.
She raised her boys, she taught them well,
A model role, if truth to tell.

The world turned round and trials tested,
And sometimes she was sadly bested;
She had to sigh and gird her will,
But proudly did she carry on with skill.

And now today she's looking pale,
She's gone as skinny as a rail.
It breaks your heart to see her thus,
But knowing her is still a plus.

And now she's stooped with eyesight bleary,
With muscles achy that make her weary,
She moves so slow, her walk's a shuffle,
It's all too much, her life's a tussle.

And now she's frail and needs much aid,
And still so little fuss she's made;
So you recall your loving days
And all of her most helpful ways.

Yet as you watch her try to sit,
Taking aim and missing it,
Her son leaps in and guides her to the chair—
It makes your heart beat everywhere.

You recall the loving years gone past,
All good memories you keep to last,
And now it's you whose face goes pale
As now you see the ghost, your loving Frail.

Did you see the lost and lonely lady
Wandering in the grocery store?
She approached a woman stocking shelves
And chatted incoherently.
Well the busy charming lady
Took her by her hands
And told her she was pretty
And how she loved her hair.
The Lost and Lonely smiled so sweetly
Pleased to be accepted so,
And as you watch the lady hug her
And kiss her on the cheek,
Then see them parting with a sigh,
Well...don't it make you want to cry?

>And you tell me that inside your world you're fine,
>That the jumpers ought to jump.
>Do you ever wonder who she used to be?
>Or what it's like for one who has forgot?

Did you see the lost and lonely lady
Wandering round about?
She has short cut white and curly hair,
Wears pearl-rimmed glasses with a flair.
She got restless, went away on walkies,
And if you meet her, she'll get a case of talkies.
She loves puppies, little kids and such...
And I miss her very much!

Did you see the lost and lonely lady
Going somewhere she's forgotten where?
She struggles to remember,
Shivers as in December,

Wand'ring here and there, with a chill inside the bone...
Well...don't it make you feel alone?

> And you tell me that in your world you're fine,
> That you've bought a brand new house;
> You've traded up your second car,
> And this year you're travelling very far.

And did you see my lost and lonely lady
Wand'ring in the street and danger?
Well the traffic stopped to let her pass—
They seemed to recognize a once bright lass.
Or did you see her wandering in the night
When the grizzled cop and partner
Picked her up and bought for her a coffee
While they scouted her identity?
They drove her to a shelter,
Told her true she was the highlight of their day,
And said they hoped that she would be okay.
Well seeing such compassion
That saw her calm as they did part,
Well...don't it go and melt your heart?

> So how can you tell me that you're fine,
> That you can afford the best of wine,
> That you can pass her and think that she'll be fine,
> And then go home with caviar and dine?

You say that you are faring very fine,
That all is right inside your world.
You say that you have got so many friends,
That you can afford to follow trends.
So let me please remind you
What it's like to not remember,

What it's like for one who has forgot.
No one wants to be the one who has forgot.

She's just a gentle lady seeking memories no longer there,
And her wandering has given me a scare.
I must find her and keep her from all danger,
And I'm so mad at me for letting her from my sight.
Won't you come and help me find her,
And save her from her plight?

> Please don't you tell me that you're fine,
> That the jumpers ought to jump.
> Please think of who this person is inside,
> Please allow for her a little pride.

———————————

Self esteem, courage,
Quiet pride, worthiness.
Dignity!

BEWARE OF FATIGUE

Fatigue is your foe, beware of his stealth,
He'll sneak up on you like an invisible ghost,
And before you know it, your willpower is toast!

For he'll creep inside of your strength
And he'll take away from your wealth
Of patience and laughter and joy.

And he'll melt your resilience
And rob you of sleep
And turn you into his toy.

He'll de-nimble your wit
Drain your talent for thought,
Then drop you right into his trap!

You will shout and you'll scream
And you'll think that you've won
But you won't know you've lost till you snap!

You'll squirm like a worm as you try to respond,
But he's robbed you indeed of all thought,
And he'll laugh, will Fatigue, for now you are caught!

So beware of that sneaky old beggar,
Never let him see that you're tired,
For you cannot scare him off with a smile.

For if you let him come into your life,
He'll wreak havoc on your physical skill,
And your health will pay a terrible bill!

When you feel that his presence is coming,
Take a deep breath and think positive things,
And choose rest over fighting his bile.

Conquer Fatigue and you've conquered your world,
Give the finger to that nasty old pest,
And take comfort you've given your best!

With Fatigue comes depression and adverse expression,
So remember the words of this boast:
Mister Fatigue is a most terrible host!

So keep up your guard and sleep your good sleeps,
Or Fatigue will guide you amiss,
And he'll dance on your grave in sheer bliss!

———————————

Easy to spot in others
Much harder to own
Dignity's essence

Oh, to have one hour alone!
To pamper and to heal my needs;
To be for a while inside my zone.
Oh how I long to be left alone.

To hear the beat of my personal drum,
To feel something other than gloomy glum,
To escape the pressure ere anger rears,
Before the Me of Myself disappears.

Oh to be able to opt right out,
With never a need for a thought to sprout,
Or have to do another one's bidding,
To live some life without the forbidding,

Away from the rattle and prattle of day,
The hustle and bustle, for this I pray.
I'd think it heaven to have such an hour;
Now where can I find me a blessed bower?

Away from TV, the tweets, the geeks,
The busy demands of the daily beats,
Away from your constantly needy needs,
And all the concerns that each of them breeds.

I urgently need to find some peace,
Where my brain can find some welcome release;
Yes I need to find some quieter place,
Far away from the madding rat race.

Somewhere to commune with my God-given soul,
To renew my spirit, that's my goal,
To refresh my psyche and wash my wit,
To rebuild my strength, refurbish my grit.

Freedom from anger, an end to stress,
Anxiety and fear and life's awful mess,
Just for a moment to feel life is clear,
Just such an hour I'd hold oh so dear.

––––––––––––––––

A Simple Little Trait

Dignity is...
A simple little trait;
If you don't have it,
It's something you can cultivate.
It's not a gift to you,
You have to earn the right,
But it's a gift that you can give
And to give is what is right;
And for the one who gets the giving,
It's a treasured way of living.

So set your dignity quite free;
Think of him or her and not of you;
It's a thing so dignified to do.

MY BUTTERFLY

I watch and I follow
From hilltop to hollow
As she flits through the garden,
Darts from flower to bower;
       She simply can't stand to be still.

She gives the cat a quick tease,
She feels fickle, without ease,
Her flight plan's in a mess,
She seems in distress,
       For she plainly can't follow a plan.

She sniffs at a rose,
Stops for a rest and a pose,
And leaves me suspended
In wonder and awe
       In the middle of a great big suppose.

Then as if newly released
She points to the east
But she flies to the north like lightning was greased
And circles right back to sniff at the rose...
       And I retreat right back to suppose.

So I suppose for her this,
And I reason re that,
Do philosophy all over the map;
How does one help to straighten her out
       Who has such a disast-er-ous plan?

Poor butterfly. My Butterfly.
I can describe her strange flight,
Enjoy her moves with delight,
I can paint all her colours,

And dismiss all my dolours,
>
But I cannot match my Butterfly.

I can imagine the sting if I damage her wing,
Imagine her gone, but that would be wrong,
So I recall how she was and the thrill and the buzz
As I follow her craziest plans,
>
And I thrill once again how I felt so alive.

So I think and I think,
To think what she thinks,
Try to feel what she feels,
Imagine the flight of her wings,
>
To get in her head and straighten her flight.

Poor butterfly, poor butterfly,
If only I could know the reason why
Of your strange flight, and of your plight,
Condemned to bedazzle...for a while...
Why can't your beauty be forever?
>
Why can't you, my poor butterfly?

But I thank you for your beauty,
I thank you for your soul,
I thank you for adventure,
I gladly pay the toll,
For the mem'ries are for ever.
And regrets? Good lord, never!

MYA

When Mya first met Daddy's Mom,
after months of change,
she knew not what to think.
Then when Grandma got into her face,
with a wide-eyed cheeky wink,
and poked at her in her odd and friendly way,
Mya thought that she was mad,
and she turned and ran away.

The next few times were touch and go
as Grandma failed at things,
and Mya stared in wonder,
if not in outright fright,
and Grandma tried and Grandma sighed
and Grandma looked so sad
as they spent their days in fits and starts
auditioning their strange new parts.

Then came the day each tried to trust,
agreed to tote as one her board of keys.
But Mya wished it here and Grandma wished it there
and the tug-o-war, like a swarm of bees,
crashed into the door, the keyboard crashed onto the floor.
So Mya, hands on hips and face of red,
had some nasty things to say, and said,
"Like you're so dumb, I wish that you were dead."

Her mother dragged her off the scene,
explained how Grandma now was kind of "old,"
and how she had been robbed of basic skill
to say the thing she wants to do or say,
'cause mem'ry failed to ring her bell.
"So please don't make a scene;

Gran has a new way now of showing love,
and now's the time for you to be the dove."

Then one day when we were going out,
Grandma's feet got stuck while getting in the car.
To our surprise and our delight,
we heard our Mya shouting out,
"I'll help Grandma, Mom."
And she got her Grandma in the car.
Then from that day on they made a pair;
to see devotion such as theirs is rare.

So they tried to play a game, with Mya saying how.
But when her Grandma didn't get the rules
Mya tried again and said, "You try it now."
So Grandma tried and Grandma mucked it up
as if the rules were made for fools,
till finally they quit and laughed it up.
Mya turned with a grown-up shrug and said,
"Sometimes Grandma gets mixed up."

Dogs and cats and silly hats
Clowns and kids galore
Mothers sipping tea and love

I THOUGHT

I thought we would grow old together
Into our happy golden years;
We'd made such full and eager plans
When we were young and strong.

We've had good times together,
Laughed and cried good tears;
We've lived full lives, obeyed our wedding banns,
And we've done nothing wrong.

We've held right tight to love's true tether,
We've survived life's strife and jeers,
Our todays still echo those Just Married rattling cans
And we still sing our favourite lovers' song.

But now you have to go, so soon before your time,
While I am left behind, our memories to mind;
Fate has caught us both, as if we both were blind,
And now I wish you peace throughout your ever time.

And I somehow will have to find a way to carry on,
For life goes on despite me; yet at tomorrow's dawn,
Somehow I still expect tomorrow's sun to shine,
And for your joie de vivre to transmute into mine.

To live with this disease
Is to have no life at all;
If you cannot be yourself
You cannot stand up tall.

And if you start to lose yourself
And feel you don't belong,
Rest assured it isn't you,
It's your disease that is so wrong.

Nor can the clever doctors learn
What it is inside your head,
Or how to talk to you in turn,
As if your memory is dead.
        Despair!

For we have failed, you and I,
To help these forlorn folk;
They've paid their dues, obeyed the rules,
And now their health is broke.

And now they're doomed to wander,
Alike but different kinds,
Lost in a fog of vagueness—
Poor souls with disconnected minds.
        Despair!

Once they were our leaders,
Their deeds indeed reflect
That while they do not ask it,
They have earned our deep respect.

And now we see them fade away,
And give them over now to care.
It's a heart-wrenching thing.

How are they going to fare?
      Despair!

And so we agonize and ask ourselves
What on earth they must be thinking?
Are they frightened all alone?
Is it that their souls are shrinking?
      Despair!

And finally we ask about this strife,
Is this the way we leave this life?
Sedated, body helpless,
Tucked inside a hospice bed,
The mind awhirl but never fed?
Unable to speak its thoughts,
Its love, to express its urgent needs?
Can they remember all their earthly deeds?
Is the mind so frustrated then
That it is still so young inside
That for the body to subside
It feels that life was just an empty lie?
      Oh Despair!

And can I forgive myself for not
Being more of comfort and of aid
To my beloved dying one?
Could I not have become more staid?
      Oh cursed despair!

And where does the mind of a dying one go
Upon the desertion of its body?
Does it truly believe that it lives on
To meet its God in body?
In what form? And will its soul go to rust? Turn to dust?

How does it reconcile that it must
Give up on all things earthly,
On family, fellow beings, partner, little ones?
On doing? Oh, to be doing!
Are there angels there a-wooing?
God let there be some angels there a-wooing.

O cruel Fate! To give us life
And fill it up with strife
And happiness and love—
Then snatch it all away.
Does it have to be so hit and miss?
How bittersweet is life's affair.
            How awful this despair!

Remind me now to cherish everything I have,
To live my life full well, not only just for me,
For I have been careless in my pothers
And I regret that I have not done well
In the realm of doing unto others.
(I'd rather have my druthers.)

Teach me to do better, please,
Teach me to conquer and to ease
This most terrible despair I've built
Around me and to free me of this guilt.

            And so begone despair.

_____

Happiness, small packages
Impish mischieve-ness
The Universe turns

GREAT PEOPLE

Or: Home Town Heroes

Society honours its own Great People,
Its leaders, its heroes, its good-deed doers,
All for good reason, it's a good thing to do,
They set good examples for us to do too.

But I have some heroes of equal worth,
Kind-hearted folk, the salt of the earth,
They're plain common folk who live in our town,
And they all deserve Good Samaritan's crown.

Like the girls in the jewellery shop in the mall,
Jewels themselves, they take her to heart.
Patient as saints they listen with care,
As my Love stutters to say what she's brought in for repair.

Like the security folk and the cops in the car
Who find her when lost from our home and afar
And bring her back home, all safe and all sound—
To them and all such we truly are bound.

Like the hospital folk, so down to earth,
They give of their time from death to birth
And take all the time that my frail one deserves—
Such is the heart of each one who serves.

Like the folks in the street when she stops them right there,
And two of them bond, an implausible pair.
Like the house retailer who listens intent,
He shows her his listings, he's heavenly sent!

Or the beggar who smiles and gives her a buck
And tells her now, dear, you'll never be stuck.

My heart wants to stop, keep this moment to mine,
Bless you my friend, may your sun ever shine.

Like the heroes inside our supportive group,
They've all been through the wringer's loop;
They come with experience and wisdom hard won,
And we soothe and support each other, each one.

And the nurses and aides and the folks in the manor
Who keep her there in a comfortable manner;
They're warm-hearted, helpful and ever aware,
So She needn't worry and I trust in their care.

These are the people of my home town,
Who help each other without a frown;
True Heroes all and deserving a hand.
May we all learn to take such a heroic stand!

———————————

Courage is as courage does
Choose your own just cause
Courage is your character

YOU SNEER TODAY

You sneer and call him doddering old fool;
Whatever happened to the golden rule?
For he can't help himself, he's only old,
It's not a sin, my son, but though it's not gold
It's Nature, going along its course.
You don't shoot him like a crippled horse.

Don't be so quick to judge, my son,
Don't count your marbles yet, you haven't won.
Listen to my wise advice to stop and think:
Learn compassion while you're in the pink.
For what you give is what you'll get;
Invest your time and pay the old fool's debt.

For when you're old and you decrepiTATE,
You'll yearn for folks to please compassionATE.

––––

Dignity
A great philosophy
Hard to practice

I am dead. I am sorry.
I'm sorry to leave this life.
It's just too much for my head,
        But to this life, I'm dead.

I'm dead because you are ill
And I must take care of you
Morning, noon and night,
        And life seems such a blight.

Not that I complain;
But it is a burden all the same,
Which I find difficult enough to carry.
        It all seems devil-sent to harry.

For I had a life like you,
Full and fulfilling,
And private and shared,
        And showing how we cared.

And though we shared life with others,
You still gave me time for me.
But no longer now;
        I no longer know how.

Friends have drifted on,
Not able to commune,
Not finding me my former lively self,
        So they've left me here up on the shelf.

For I have become you in my caring,
And you have become a shadow
Of the former vibrant, younger you,
        Bubbling and fresh as newly perking brew.

So now that I don't have a friend,
No time at all for me,
No longer is there we, no longer two,
    We've become a single you.

And so "I" am dead. I'm sorry.
All I do is worry.
It all spins inside my head,
    And now the I of Me is dead.

––––––––––––

Man not feeling fine?
Cloudy skies confirm the mood?
Lady smile, sunshine

YOU CAN'T WIN

She was in the ninth stage of her gingerly state
And feeling quite touchy and easily upset,
So the contrary side of her love was displayed...
And the cool of my jokes could no longer be played.

Well I tried and I tried and I darn nearly died
Trying to live up to the knot I had tied;
But science dictates that inside nuptials' din
That you, you poor blighter, simply can't win.

Answer the door, she asked when it knocked,
Sure, said I, what is it the door wants to know?
She flung a bowl and I took fast flight...
And I slept on the couch that night.

Once she asked why didn't you tell me all that?
I quipped that the subject had never come up.
She snarled and I said I thought we were tight...
And I slept on the couch that night.

Well I sought to make up, I offered her peace,
But the more I dug in, the greater increase
Of the gingerly action and the awful sight
Of the couch where I slept that night.

I slept on the couch, and I slept on the couch,
And I wiggled and squiggled and squirmed,
I thought about what I had said without gain,
And I swore not to say that again.

But the very next day, my penchant for word play
Sent me back to sleep on the couch,
For I swear to you this, that my tongue has wings,
And that darned old couch needs new springs.

You might say that I never do learn,
That I'm a beggar for punishment;
But whatever the case, and it might be a sin,
With a partner in a gingerly state you can't win.

She split the house chores and she did her full share
As I struggled to polish the hob,
But I made it a gaffe when I called it a blight...
And I slept on the couch that night.

I went out on the town to relax my old bones,
And she said it was Parliament's Act to tell;
I said it's My Act to act and that's my delight...
And I slept on the couch that night.

So I told myself this, you might as well grin
'Cause you know you're not going to win,
For try as you might you'll never be right,
And you'll sleep on the couch tonight.

You might say that I never do learn,
That I'm a beggar for punishment,
But whatever the case, and it might be a sin,
With a partner in such a gingerly state, you can't win.

Now you may think she's an awful tear;
Usually, though, she has no trouble to bear
My smart-alecky ways. But in this gingerly state
My smart-alecky remarks are pure bait.

Darned if a man can get anything right
To please his woman, try as he might,
Better to learn to sleep like Snow White...
'Cause you're gonna sleep on the couch tonight.

Then one day with a kiss on my cheek she said,
When opportunity calls, you should give it a smile,
So I gave her my widest big grin of delight...
And we slept on the couch that night.

Oh we slept on the couch, yes we slept on the couch,
We slept, I said slept, on the couch that night,
For when the wind blows so strong to the south,
You can't look a gift horse in the mouth.

———————————————

Silent, angels wing above
Clumsy, people thrash about
Animals get on

A LIGHTER MOMENT

Grandparents' day, down at the seniors' home,
With spinning wheels and games and prizes
And throngs of happy visiting relations;
At every turn you could be taken by surprises.

But when she sought me out inside the crowd,
Her face was full of smiling laughter,
She said to "Come and see, I'll show you. I'll show you."
I couldn't wait to see the answer. Not if it came the faster.

And she took me firmly by my willing hand
And led me down the hall around the corner,
And on toward the big blank wall inside the sporting hall,
And gestured proudly at the foreigner.

"Look," she said, with gleeful, hearty laughter,
"There she is, that woman. There she is, that woman."
Look I did, and there she was indeed. Indeed. With me.
There she was, herself, that lovely laughing woman.

I cherished all her laughter, and I revelled in her joy,
For lighter moments such as these had grown to be so few.
So we waved right back at them, the couple's image laughing there,
And thus we thanked "that woman" for this happiness anew.

One day while stocking up on groceries,
She wanted chocolate for the wee grandkids.
I said their parents did not allow them sweets.
She tried again while in the pay-out line,
And gently I reminded her.
Storming now, she strode away somewhere apart,
Leaving me in awe beside the grocery cart.

After I had paid the bill, I looked around,
But she was not right there, nor anywhere.
I parked the cart and scoured all the rows,
She simply wasn't there. I looked outside—
Sometimes she paced the great outdoors,
Shooting steam, quite mad enough to scream.
I feared the fate of her too hot blood stream.

I asked security and they went out to look.
I called police and told them she was gone.
They entered her into their Missing Book,
Told me to wait right there in case she did come back.

Anxious minutes dragged on by;
Heavy hung the question why.
But she it seems was on the fly.
I told myself I ought to die.

A cop car finally drove up to me;
I stepped right up for him to see,
But as I did I glimpsed across the lot:
Security's good lady coming back
With Her in tow and chatting forth and back,
"I found her over there," the lady said,
"She was talking sweet with two wild dogs.
I swear those killer dogs were listening in."

How, I wonder, how those dogs would know. Well gee!
How strange, an animal with ESP.

She came with me as calm as calm can be
And we collected all our grocery.
Then she told me of those nice wild dogs.
Well! Let me tell you true, the mind, it bogs!

Innocence is pure
Innocence is self-defence
Innocence is smile

Behold this weary woman wan and worn,
Her wishes dead on duty's vine, yet still she plies
Her tender loving care upon her ailing man forlorn.
Ever now but half-awake, it's plaintively she cries,
    "Oh, to sleep until I wake."

Until at last from nursing toil she's broken down,
Her body aches, her mind attends his wake.
So full of strife, she lays her body down
And weeps. In anguish then she wails "For pity's sake,
    Let me sleep until I wake."

And such a load is the heavy load that's mine,
Like hers, my nerves do tread a tattered line,
My strength is fading, my will is weak,
And I dream of escaping this weary streak,
    And I cry, "to sleep until I wake."

But her needs are great, much greater than are mine,
And while I dream those dreams of that bed of mine,
And I try so hard and I try not to break,
She needs my care, and I know what's at stake,
    And I cry, "Oh, to sleep until I wake."

And so that lady who fought the disease
In her husband for nigh on twenty years,
Rediscovered herself in her burden's release,
And couldn't stop smiling for twenty more years,
    For now she sleeps until she wakes.

And as for me, I hope to attain
Some of that peace, and also gain
The rich full fullness of a full waking day,
And a taste of freedom that lets me say,
    "I can sleep until I wake."

WHERE HAVE I GONE?

One day we thought we'd lost the television zapper,
We searched the whole house through.
Then in jest I said I bet she put it in the freezer,
And though I'm just a geezer, this turned out to be the truth.
We laughed a lot and kidded her, though much to her chagrin,
Till even she gave in, and flashed her trademark cheeky grin.

Then one day she forgot the name of her dearest, oldest friend.
We wondered, what that meant, but so of course did she,
So in our minds we scurried, and then we played a silly game
To reverse her soulful "I am worried," despite our "what's there in a name?"
Till she recalled the ID of that same and dearest friend,
And life resumed its same old scat, each day another blend.

Then one day she lost her way while simply coming home,
And when at last we found her, just wandering in the road,
She'd forgot the milk but she had bought three more bags of buns.
She laughed it off and joked that she was thinking of some other things;
We shared a thought that thoughts must fly on silken wings, you see.
But still she said, "I am concerned, how anxious need I be?"

But no longer could she sort the spoons, and filed the forks with knives,
And when I tried to help her sort, she sniffed with peeved denial,
She walked away and left the chores, in short, strictly up to me.

I tried to soothe her worried mind, to give it one more trial,
She signed that life's a grind and said, "I don't feel free."
And then with doleful eyes she asked, "What is happening to
me?"

When she tried to cook a meal, as once she always did,
First for seven, then for five, and then for just we two,
She found the chore confounding—confusion was
compounding,
She stood with frying pan in hand, the other held a cup,
Her thoughts askew she never knew the answer to "What's
up with you?"
And sadly in bewilderment she said, "I don't know what to
do."

Once upon a meal that I had cooked, for me a special feat,
She did well until the end, when I had to spear the beet.
Then quirkily a change of pace, with one dramatic pause,
She went fishing for the past at the bottom of a vase.
Helplessly she looked at me, a lost and lonely fawn,
In desperation then she asked, "Where do you think I've
gone?"

We had to put her in a home, where, I'm very sad to say,
Her mind would wander in and out and I would have to
guess,
"Are you in Olde England now, or are you living in the
West?"
She looked at me with mindful stare and asked me, "What's
your name?"
Long since that she'd forgotten hers, all memories awry,
And with a wistful sigh she asked me then, "Who am I?"

We nursed her long, we nursed her kind, she didn't seem to mind,

But came the day in a visit there, she cast the oddest mindful stare,

And for a flash her Self of old was back and fully full aware—
And with her famous cheeky grin and trademark twinkling eye,

She found the voice of former Self, the one from years by-gone,

And wryly cracked her one last little joke. She said, "I'm gone!"

Red hawk flying high
People living unaware
Gopher digging deep

As I watched her suffer pain and weary of all sympathy,
I felt forlorn, my mood was torn, 'tween anger and of empathy;
I could not fix her ills, there was no healing voice,
And search as hard as search I could, I still could find no choice.

I could not live in such a state depressed
Without a way for happiness to be expressed;
I lived in fear that I'd embrace misanthropy;
There was no doubt, I gravely needed therapy.

And so I joined like-minded minds and found some sympathy,
And now my world with rough and smooth is like a little symphony;
I say my pain in rhyme and pass it off without a fee:
I read it to the group and walk away quite free!

In sum, I find my path to peacefulness is this:
Accept my fate and fight her fight to cure all this.

Fruit bowl full of fruit
Bowl of dark mahogany
Appetite brewing

I HEARD A SONG TODAY

I heard a song today
It made me think of you
The singer sang of love
I no longer felt so blue

Today I saw a daffodil
It made me think of you
The daffy was your flower
A sign of life's return anew

I heard a song today
So full of melody's sweet hue
The kind you always used to hum
And of course it made me think of you

I heard a song today
Of things that ring so true
It spoke of days gone by
It made me think of you

Yes I heard a song today
A haunting song of rain and dew
Of children, puddles, puppies' play
It made me think of you

I heard a song of flowers
The words still haunt my mind
They made me think of you
The way things always do

So I sing a song today
I sing a song for you
It says that I love you
I'll sing that every day

The road was hard,
The battle bitter,
And though you proved indeed
To be a worthy foe,
Your cause was wrong,
Your tactics merely spite,
And she it was who fought
The better bitter fight.

You can steal her memory,
And even take her life,
But you cannot erase
Her many helpful deeds,
For all good works by her
Already have been done:
So you have lost the war,
Already she has won!

So you may wrack her body,
But you can never take her soul,
For the "She" remains complete,
And you shall pay the toll.
For she's the proven Victor,
And to the Victor comes the peace,
And she shall dance with angels,
And wear the Golden Fleece!

HOPE 2

So be faithful to Hope, there's no need to grope
In the darkness of fear and despair;
Smile at adversity, your smile will beget smiles
And you will enjoy each moment you're gifted.
For when you can feel that your heart has been lifted
You'll see that Hope has travelled you miles.
For who needs the strife that the worry begets,
It will only prevent you from winning the fight
And sap the resources you need to hold tight
And to put in and get out the best of yourself.
So draw on your strength and your inner reserve
And remember that Hope is always right there;
She's ready to help and she's waiting for you,
And remember that Hope is your prayer.

Teardrops fall as love
Laughter mocks the weak
White dove flies in hope

I see your broken body—
But I see your spirit shining through—
And how I do admire
How your love remains so true.

I see you there inside your broken shell,
I see your soul and what your eyes can tell,
And I will ring the bell proclaiming that you're there,
Still living, loving, there inside your broken shell.

I will protect you now, Love,
And keep all harm away from you,
And know I love you dearly;
Know, my Love, how much I care.

I know somehow that still you dare,
That somehow deeply still you care
For Life, there inside your broken shell,
And I will strive to tell the world
How wonderful a soul you are,
Even now from there, inside your broken shell.

I see true beauty lies there deep within
And not upon the outer shell,
Beauty of the shell can shatter like a spell,
But your spirit's strong and you will live to win.

I see your broken body,
But I see your spirit shining through,
And how I do admire
How your love remains so true.

IV. Late Stages and the Home

There she sits, yet sleek in her design,
Marred some say by life's odd scrape and bump,
Looking sad though still with life within,
Trying to cope with life upon the dump.

Once I raced the best of them, she sighed,
I was a winner among the greats;
Now that I'm older they think I'm through
And they throw me on the old scrapheap.

Life upon the scrapheap ain't so grand,
In this place there's nothing much to do;
People come and sadly shake their heads
And they whisper things like poor old you.

It doesn't help, the sympathy,
It doesn't bring me back.
I wish I could re-start again,
I'd beat you on the track.

There she sits with life that's still within,
No way left to play life's game again,
With thoughts no use though thoughts run deep,
It cuts cross-grain, life on the old scrapheap.

Alas, she sighs, I see you there,
I see you want to help.
If only I could speak again,
You and I'd elope!

And I stand beside, I cannot hide,
As I deeply weep for her within
That fate and she had to collide
And land her in the scrapheap bin.

I turn and go with heavy sigh
For our heady days that run so deep,
I rue the day they towed her away
And dumped her on that old scrapheap.

Scrap metal rusting
Dry stalks blowing in dry breeze
Small bird is nesting

Goodbye my love, farewell for now,
Although you left me years ago.

An alien came and filled your skin
And shunted you aside.

I know you live, alive and well,
Just too deep inside to reach.

It's so unfair what that alien's done
To masquerade as you.

I search for you, I reach for you,
But it's the alien looking back.

So goodbye for now, my love,
Until we pass, and soon we'll meet again.

———————

Country, boy, river
Blue sky, soft wind, forest green
Red Wing Blackbird sings

LIFE IN A FOLKS' HOME

Sleeping forms, stooped and bent,
Weakened limbs from lack of use,
Moaning, crying, a curse or two,
Life clings on through life's abuse.

They suffer through till dinner time,
They eat from spoons that others hold;
They tolerate the toileting,
The bedding down by nurses bold.

The minds are fading, the eyes lose sparkle,
The body-life is slowly fading;
The twinkle that once was them
Is losing its once more subtle shading.

So they sit and wait, dreaming dreams,
Silently reliving their old-time stories,
Adventures that they cannot speak,
Inner pictures of former glories.

To witness this most painful, dark descent—
Torture for the poor old residents,
Lamentation for my poor old watching self—
Is to admit 'gainst life's assaults, they've no defence.

If only science could end disease,
If only life could end with ease
And stop this woe upon us all...
An ideal world, a dream for all.

As I sit at the window, looking out,
I see people passing by,
Cars coming, cars going, cars parking still,
People coming in, people going out,
People, people, coming, going,
And here I sit...I can only sigh!

I see the sun, the clouds, the breeze in the trees,
I see rain, I see crowds, I see buzzing bees;
Those folks are doing, going, seeing...

And me? I sit here, and I see these four walls,
I see curtain panels, I hear gasps,
And sighs, and moans and groans
All around me, nurses dashing here, dashing there,
Visitors coming, visitors going,
People from the outside air...

My mind sprawls, and I, I have so few stimuli...
And I sit, and I wait, and I sit, and I stare...
And time chugs slowly on...as the world passes by.

I sit and I see but I cannot do.
Yesterday I saw the mountains.
Today I see the rain.
People hike on the mountains.
Children play in the rain.
City folk bustle and country folk hustle...

The world turns on its axis
And it turns right round me
As I sit here at my hospice window pane...

The world is passing me by...

DIGNITY IN CARE

Dignity in care is a calling indeed
It's pride in yourself, giving pride where it's not

It's guiding her on her difficult path
Understanding and easing her lot

It's dressing her daily in her own good clothes
For the pride in her looks that she's always sought

Privacy granted while giving a bath
Assistance discreetly to sit on the pot

It's to notice whenever a person needs help
And giving it willingly, not that you ought

It's keeping your person in care always clean
From the top to the bottom, wash every spot

It's watching for signs and distress in her mien
Keeping her comfy, not too cold or too hot

Talking to her as you pass by her chair
And keeping her secrets and never to plot

It's touching her hand whenever you can
And making quite sure she's never forgot

It's a pat on the shoulder, a shawl for her warmth
To remind her, her life was never for naught

It's to do unto others as you'd do unto you
It's doing what Grandma and the Bible has taught

It's a gift that you give to your person in need
And in the so doing, dignity's wrought

Dignity in care is a duty well served
It's caring with care, it's doing with thought

Its rewards are abundant, its feelings are great
You'll sail on love's air in a virtual yacht

And the person you care for will love you for that
Dignity in care, it's the best that you've got

———————

Flitting spirit free
Hanging basket, barren tree
Butterfly plant, home

VISITING HOUR

If you can spare one hour in the pub,
or two inside with films, aye, here's the rub,
you can spend that hour, maybe even two,
visiting your ailing one, the hour that she's due.

And if you have the time to sit out in the blazing sun
thinking on the beauty of your alabaster skin,
you have the time to sit with him, whose illness is no sin,
to fill the emptiness, and avoid a thoughtless shun.

Think of her just lying lost and lonely in that bed,
where time ticks by and outside life never sees inside her
head,
where she lies pregnant with the wait on waiting's painful
pace,
picture disappointment then—the picture is her face!

If you can while away your time in the worry of it all,
and fret about what some day may upon you possibly befall,
remember that the giving time is better than resenting,
and loving bears more fruitful seeds than any vain
begrudging.

If you can spend an hour painting up your pretty face
so you will look your very best when you go stepping out,
you can spare an hour cheering one who's in a sickness
bout,
and losing time is really never going to be the case.

Think of him just lying there, feeling lost inside that bed,
where he lies expectantly through all of waiting's painful
pace
where time ticks by and life outside never walks into his
head,
picture disappointment then—the picture is his face!

But if you choose to spend your pub time extra dollar
instead upon a bouquet, or simply on one flower,
you'll turn her day to sweetness, if only for a while;
well, sweetness lingers and will give her hour style.

If upon a latte you can spare yourself the time to drift,
you can spend an hour with one whose health is down upon
his luck;
and I promise you that you will never ever miss that buck,
for the time you freely give to him is a lover's greatest gift.

Yes you can stop your life for just one hour;
yes you are strong and yes you have that power
to spend that hour to lift another's spirits up—
to fill the other half of her almost half-drained cup.

Yes it's visiting hour, that's what that hour is called,
relief from all those boring hours that crawled
as she yearns for you and for your treasured hour
to ease her ache with love—your time's her sweetest hour.

HERE'S WHAT I DID TODAY

I visited my loved one today, in the nursing home,
Where now she lives, in her inner zone,
And she smiled when I wiggled my brows,
So I whispered a repeat of our wedding vows.

But today was a challenge, though I live in hope,
For through it all, I manage to cope.
For I remember the centremost piece
Of wise advice that gives me new lease:
"I can be right or be at peace."
For it isn't I but she who never gets ease,
Nor is it her, it's this damned disease
That put her here in this awful state—
And I am sworn to serve as her faithful mate.

Oh I admit I did not want to go,
It broke up my day and filled me with woe,
And to see her like this engendered fear
And I had to fight to bring courage near
And trudge my way to the nursing home
And try to read her like a medical tome,
And to keep my legs from wanting to roam.
I had so many things I wanted to do,
And through her long struggle, I'd done so few.

But when I got there and approached her chair,
I knew ten reasons why I should be there,
For her hand reached out and her voice greeted me
And she gripped my hand and leaned her head on me
And instantly we were bonded as a single "we,"
And to see her face light up and to see her smile
Made my heart beat a hundred mile,

So I was happy I'd defeated my sorry woe,
And I'm ever so glad I decided to go.

Now I lay me down upon our wedding bed,
Feeling alone but without any dread,
For she is in comfort without any pain,
And I know I'll see her tomorrow again.

———————————

Shave and a haircut
No one even notices
What good vanity?

SOMETHING ABOUT HER

She lives in a wheelchair and can't even speak
And nothing in life can be seen to be fair,
But something about her makes your interest peak,
For she draws you right in and you want to be there.

There's something about her that draws people's love,
Some cosmic attraction, a magnetic distraction
That melts your resistance with childlike insistence
That says you're in love, and, of course, this attraction
Just fits like a glove, and it's too late, my friend,
You can't help but to purr. To resist now just does not occur,
And you're as helpless as kittens and babies and all,
And she leaves you good karma and smiling in awe.

It could be her eyes or her winsome, sweet smile;
Could be she looks wise, or her absence of guile.
Whatever it be, it's pure love's sweet little nip,
And it's no use to fight it, you're locked in its grip.

The people all love her, her family dotes,
If a contest were held, she'd win all the votes.
There's something about her that you cannot define,
You have to surrender and try to refine.
There's something about her that makes you feel fine.

Yes there's something about her that draws you right in,
Something that's pure and that speaks of no sin;
It's a charm that's so easy that sends no alarm,
And you want to protect her and keep her from harm.

Trotting up and down the lane ways,
as if we'd done this always.
Trot-trot trot-trot trot-trot...
Trotting down her mem'ry lanes,
she feels the breeze again
from all the fresh outdoors,
the breeze upon her face
reminding her of freedom's ways,
reliving all her lead-foot days!

Trot-trot trot-trot trot-trot...

Remembering all the chirping of the crickets
as she ran so freely through the grass;
eight years old and life's a lucky pass.

Trot-trot trot-trot trot-trot...

Down the lane way with a lane way pass
people look askance,
people smile and give a happy glance
as my gleeful passenger
laughs a happy laugh
and waves a sign to me
with cool air in her face
to please increase my pace.

Trot-trot trot-trot trot-trot...

My footsteps rhythmic as a rickshaw boy's,
Trot-trot trot-trot trot-trot...

Each ride a chariot ride.
Oh, the freedom of it all,
and she laughs with utter joy

hee-hee hee-hee hee-hee
Wheeeeee!

Watch for Policeman
with his radar gun.
Hee-hee hee-hee hee-hee!
Oh, the thrill!

Remembering with glee,
till she had so many speeding tickets
she traded licence plates with me;
and I went to court for her,
and we won!
Hee-hee hee-hee hee-hee!

Trot-trot trot-trot trot-trot...

Oh, the thrill!
Trot-trot trot-trot trot-trot...
Footsteps down her memory lane...

Rickshaw boy,
Chariot ride.

Trot-trot trot-trot trot-trot...
Wheeeeeeeeeeeeeeee!

I show her books of faded photographs,
memories from all our former paths,
of times when she and I were young
and life was always joyous "Ships Ahoy!"
and times among our kids, when they were full of joy.
I sing the songs that we have always sung,
And she recalls her former playful ways...
and she cries for all her yesterdays.

She cries for now she has so few tomorrows left
and no longer can she serve; bereft,
she laments this stage of age,
for she has much more that she can give.
But her memory's become a sieve,
although some scenes are just a stage
and some todays are but replays...
she cries for all her yesterdays.

At times there's nothing else to do but rage
against this wretched prison cage
and try to say what's in her mind.
But still she knows the joys of how to live,
it's in her altruistic need to give,
a testament of how one can be kind
in the face of hardships in a maze...
and so she cries for all her yesterdays.

Old photos, familiar melodies,
a kiss, a tender touch, all remind her of so much;
her face then crinkles up as if she prays...
and she weeps for all her yesterdays...

GRIEF UNEXPECTED

I walked into the florists, some daffodils to buy,
But when I found a sales girl, my eyes began to cry.
Now where that grief had come from I really couldn't say,
Excepting that the daffodil will always make her day.

I thought I was prepared to handle this small task;
But it was just too much to handle, far too much to ask,
For thinking of her languishing, never to return,
Sudden grief attacked me, and sudden grief can burn.

Forlorn I paced around that florist's aromatic rows.
Because the daffodil is proof of how my fondness grows,
I sighed and breathed and paced until I staunched those
tears,
Because I knew that daffodils would surely staunch her fears.

Sometimes life just happens, but this was Mothers' Day,
And "I love you" is what I wanted daffodils to say.

Feel soothing softness
Sandpaper abrasiveness
Kind word working out

My honeyed one she lives upon a chair with wheels;
She spends her days in mindless thought,
Where once she'd spread the joy inhabiting her zeal.
For better days she's paid and bought.

I went into the nursing home to visit her
And nearly wept to see her thus;
I smiled my brightest smile and tried so hard to purr
And not to weep or make a fuss.

I sang to her and wheeled her on several little trips,
To live again our former miles;
My honey took my hand and pressed it to her lips
To kiss it tenderly with smiles.

I remembered all she'd done in life
That now she cannot do;
I saw how that for her was strife
And made her very blue.

She'd given oh so much with nothing in return;
I wracked my brain to find a cure—
And so I found her love of choc'late still did burn,
And that it helped her to endure.

Now if she's sad and dreams of freedom's chariots,
I know the thing that I must do,
Henceforth my honey she shall have those choc-o-lates
That soothe her very soul so true.

When she has her choc'lates, her eyes get up and dance,
She lives her life as one who's freed.
Now her wants and needs are met, life is now enhanced,
Now we know, choc'late is her creed.

And if today she wants a whiskey or a rum,
There is no fuss, there is no muss;
Nor is there if she opts to sit around and hum,
Or if she feels the need to cuss.

Freedom is as freedom does, freedom is the Might,
And surely she has earned the right
To live her final years with brightest of éclat—
So let her eat her choc-o-lat!

Living on cloud nine
Rainbows, ribbons, all is fine
Sweet, dark chocolate

She flitters and she flutters,
She dithers and she bothers,
And frantically she pothers,
And poor thing she never knows why.

I try to be helpful,
I try to be artful,
I try to ease her on through,
So she won't cast a troublesome die.

And so we sit together,
Make believe forever,
Trying to forget all other,
For "they" have other fish to fry.

We try not to let it bother,
She calls it dumb old clobber,
We try to laugh at Fate,
Pretend a finger in his eye.

And when it's time to part,
Neither one will dart,
Too much pain to start,
And so it is we sit and sigh.

For this we know quite fully well,
That only time will tell,
And tomorrow we will sit again,
Thankful that today we will not die.

A NEW KIND OF LOVE

At first it was passion,
Obsession,
and then,
enduring love,
maintaining love.

Also frustrating love,
as in I hate your action, but I still love you...

Followed by the grand-parenting
with renewed youthfulness
and giving love elsewhere

until...
dementia,
with all its challenges,
disbeliefs, denials,
realignments,
readjustments,
tears and anguish—
even pissed-off and outright angry
moments

and then,
in care...

Thinking back,
I'd always wondered why the old folks homes.
Then, in her dementia, toward the tired end,
I began to see why.
Now: while, as a man, I'd always had the charge of care,
old-fashioned as I am,
but,
this is different.

Now she needs...
total care!

And it is so endearing,
somehow,
strangely,
when she greets me with tears
of gladness and relief and hope,
and she is so dependent on me,
and so loving...

it has taught me a new kind of love,

a kind of tender tenderness
I'd never known before;
a new kind of laughter, together,
even, somehow, a new kind of peace...

I guess those who said
that caring for one in care
was a privilege and a love
were not so crazy as I'd thought

for in this trial one does indeed grow
and learn that service is indeed
an honour and a calling...
and then I remember
that one lonely day
it may be me who needs the care,
and I will crave to have
someone else to share
my burden
and to comfort me.

And I will try to remember,
at first, it was a passion...

keep the home fire burning
for every life keeps on turning...

———————

Loneliness is hard
Life inserts its busy head
Company can cure

Trot-trot-trotting
free for freedom's sake.
Slow it down to pass the station
here on Main,
then trot-trotting down the lane,
free air in curly hair,
rider squeals with glee,
"Look at me, look at me."

Tuh-weeeeeeet!
Dreaded whistle blows:
Policeman with his radar gun!
holds up his palm-leaf-sized hand
to bring me to a skidding halt.
His very presence screams "my fault!"

BUSTED!

"No running in the halls.
Someone may pop out
and you will crash.
Think of your rider."

I hang my head,
ashamed that I was caught.
Sorry, because my rider
had so enjoyed the ride.

"Understand?" Policeman asks,
scowling beneath a beetle brow.
"Yes nurse," I say,
and meekly walk my ride
back down the hall,
careful to steer her wheelchair

around the nursing aid
coming out the patient's door.
Obedient to the core.

I look back and nurse is outta sight...
then I scoot down the hall
at my very fastest walk,
hips a-wag, as if one's hips could talk,
and my rider squeals with glee
Tee-hee tee-hee tee-hee!

Freedom is as freedom does.
No running in the hall.

———————————

Sleeping cat at peace
Small boy playing ball
Convergence waits ahead

It's said the knight in armour
　　　Picked the flower for his love;
He did to prove his ardour,
　　　But he wasn't any dove,
For his armour weighed him down
　　　Into the river though he fought,
He tossed the posy as he drown,
　　　Crying please forget me not!

Weedy little flower, perky in its purple,
You stand for memory and precious love so true,
Your petals five are symbols showing that you care,
Your golden heart a sign of love willingly laid bare.

Five pretty little petals,
Held by a heart of gold;
One petal stands for true love,
As beauteous as the dove;
Another is devotion,
Embracing love's emotion;
A third is hope to help you cope,
A fourth is caring care,
With courage to be there,
While number five is memory
To honour you and me.

Chorus:
Forget-me-not, Forget-me-not,
Pretty purple and splendid, little flower.
Forget-me-not, Forget-me-not,
Remembrance is your power.

And while you may be going,
Your spirit lives with me.

Our memories are as beauteous
As any living tree.
So I promise this to you,
With everything I've got,
That I'll be true dear,
That I'll forget you not.

The whole is like a star,
The symbol of a dream.
It stands for love that flows,
As does the laughing stream.
So wear the little flower,
The wee Forget-me-not,
It is the flower of remembrance
And love's forever-ever knot.

It is love, remember-ance,
A forever-ever knot.
The flower of remember-ance,
The wee Forget-me-not.

Chorus

Who will visit her if I'm not here?
Who will hold her quite so dear?

Who will comfort her in times of need?
Who can honour her with love's own creed?

What girl guide or what boy scout
Will come to her with care devout?

If I'm not here will she not grieve?
Is there someone else here to believe?

I worry that she'll live in fear
That no one else will shed a tear.

Who has time to care for others?
Who else cares like their own mothers?

Who will visit her if I'm not here?
Who will hold her quite so dear?

THE BOARDS OF LIFE

Together we trod the boards of life,
Together we tread this stage,
Together we grew and together we age,
We travel together as man and wife.

I lost my freedom when she lost hers,
All after a life of furs and burs,
For now in a prison of angst she lives
In confusion that never forgives.

And now as she sinks into a void,
I'm left alone and cold to the bone;
I angst so far from my comfort zone,
Though I know no spirit can be destroyed.

She tries to break free, her angst forbidden,
I try to cope, I feign no fear,
I try to listen, I try to hear,
But try as I will, I am still angst-ridden.

Ahhh...
But, now that I think it all over,
She was always my lucky clover;
I devoutly resolve to angst no more:
We were blessed from each other's core.

Together we tread the boards of life,
Together we'll tread this stage,
Together we'll stay to the end of our age,
Together we'll travel as man and wife.

Do not sing this siren's evil song
Her words do cut like laser sword
Resist, resist, for pity's sake

She will seduce you 'ere too long
If you should dally in her sward
Do not sing this devil's evil song

You do not have to go along
Defy, defy her tempting chord
Resist, resist, for future's sake

You do so know the right from wrong
You do so know how eagles soared
Do not sing this siren's tempting song

You can learn to sing a better song
Do not adopt her as your lord
Resist, resist, for honour's sake

Gird your loin and practise to be strong
Or she will sing upon your wake
Do not sing this siren's devil song
Resist, resist, for pity's sake

AN ANGEL WHISPERED

I knelt beside her grave, alone and lost,
Not knowing how to grieve,
Not able to believe,
For life had dealt us two its double-cross.

I scanned the tombstone garden, heard the sound
As others seemed to cope,
But still I found no hope,
For wrapped in chains of grief I still was bound.

I went into the chapel there and knelt.
I tried to pray, I wept
for all the love I kept,
But try and try, no solace there I felt.

But just as I gave up on life so dear,
A voice, all faint and new,
Came clear, and then I knew,
For I heard an angel whisper in my ear.

"Do not despair," she seemed to say, "your path is clear,
Though Love's no longer here,
Her spirit lingers near,
With thanks for keeping up your vows so dear."

That angel's voice did soothe my nerves somehow,
And now I have the strength
To live my breadth and length
And I will be so much the stronger now.

Yes I heard an angel whisper in my ear,
I've nothing now to fear;
I walk in peace. I shed no tear.
For I heard an angel whisper in my ear.

SERENITY

Serenity for most is but a dream:
Serenity would be the cream
Atop the Milk of Human Kindness.

For it's a skill you have to will and hone,
Until it breathes all on its own
And you become the essence of the Zen of Calm.

Serenity seems like a touch of God,
A steady hand on a stabling rod
That guides you on to a State of Harmony.

But believe in God, or if you can't,
It matters not, unless you rant,
For it will help you breathe the Spirit of the Peace.

Then come what may it's here to stay,
For the more you live this way
The more the slings and arrows just roll off your back.

For serenity is here for all,
It helps us all to stand up tall,
And kindness is as kindness does, and so we live Serene.

LUCKY ONE

Oh, I have been the lucky one
To have lived and learned with her,
For always it was she,
The happy, doing one,
The giving, caring soul.

Our life has been,
Since those giddy, happy times,
A story of adventure,
One of give and take
And always and for 'ever'
Love for each and other's sake.

How lucky to have met her,
How marvelous she cared.
Forever will I wonder
Why it was she dared
To have belief in me.
But whatever was the mystery,
Always I will cherish
The faith that both we shared
Through our lifelong span together—
So happy we were paired.

And I am not complaining,
Indeed I'm giving thanks,
For what I've gained from what she gave
Would enrich, I think, all of Britain's banks.

And now when she is fading,
And I reflect upon our past,
I see the longer shadow,
The one that she has cast.

She's the one whose anima
Was the light that guided me;
And now that I am old and she is gone,
I'll try to shine as she has shone.

And so it's ever thanks to her
I've been that very lucky guy,
To have lived and loved with her,
The giving, caring soul,
Who never asked me why.

———————

Orange ball
Whirling wind
Blazing son

TO THE CAREGIVER

I sing to you oh caring, giving nurse,
I thank you, doctor, for your healing ways,
I praise you caregivers, equal in your worth,
Who, for our frails, become vanguard mainstays.
Though sometimes abused in varying ways
While walking in shoes of your patient's mile,
You cry for your charge in your caring ways,
Yet through it all you can teach us to smile.

Nurses are angels and doctors are saints,
Caregivers are lovers without restraints.
They all administer without complaints.
Wretched me, not worthy to kiss their hem,
Helpless in the shadow of each such gem...
And oh, if ever I could be like them!

Folk singer, folk singer sing,
Sing for the folks do,
Sing with your heart, sing with soul.

AFTER ALL IS SAID AND DONE

After you have done it all
and said all you have to say,

after serving best you could,
and you'd gladly serve again,
       'cause you never thought of gain,

and you've said your deepest prayers
and you've said your soothing words,
helped the ones you love in deed
       'cause it was their hour of need,

and after all your actions spoke
even louder than your words,
all your actions led to good,
and erased the need to fight,
       'cause what you stood for was right,

And you bore your losses well
and learned your lessons from,
given till you'd nothing more,
lived your life with love to spare,
       'cause your standard was to share,

after you have shared and cared,
were so weary, worn and scared
in your body, mind, and soul,
       'cause virtue takes its toll,

and you have faced all dangers,
and paid the cost of living,
       'cause you believe in giving,

Then after all is said and done,
you can say that you have won!

The Big Wig who walked up and down the ranks and files
with the officers inspecting the cadet troops
...that was her.
The woman taking the salute on the dais during the march
past at the inspection
...that was her.
That lady up on deck with the admiral at the sail past
...that was her.
The woman who founded two cadet corps and guided them
to fruition
...that was her.
That woman who busts my buttons I'm so proud
...that is her.

The woman who outsold the men in real estate in Hamilton
...that was her.
The woman who outsold the men in London's medical
journals
...that was her.
The woman who raised our three sons
...that was her.
The woman who worked three jobs while I was away
...that was her.
The woman who captured my heart at our first dance step
...that was her.
The woman who saved me from nothingness
...that was her.
The woman I most adore
...that, my friend, is her.

In saying final goodbye—Monarch leaves every fall for gigantic migration, to breed, lay, die. Life is so transitory.

Flitting past in erratic flight,
A colorful pair of wings—
Fascinating beauty.
You want to grab her and keep her.
But fragile and helpless,
The butterfly squeezes your finger
And looks a pleading look in your eye.
"Please don't hurt me,"
She seems to be saying,
And somehow something touches your soul,
For the butterfly seems to be kin
With the fragility of soul
That inhabits your being.

If you net her, you will injure her,
If you keep her in a glass tank
You will starve her,
Even with the best of intentions
And care.

No. Let the butterfly fly.
Her life is so short.
Her job is to spread beauty and hope,
Her colours are colours of love,
And mercy must leave her to live.
Yes, let the butterfly fly,
Let the butterfly fly...
And when it's time to let her go—
You will know when it is time—
Let the butterfly fly.

The butterfly must go her butterfly way;
Her time is all but used up.
The butterfly must fly to butterfly land,
It's time to let her go.
Her beauty will live forever
And nourish your soul,
It's time to let your Butterfly fly.
Let your Butterfly fly.

Give your heart away
All for love of Butterfly
Troubled soul at rest

Forget me not, for I'm still here,
Please don't fear for me;

But remember me, remember us,
Please don't make a fuss.

We had good times, remember them,
Remember me, remember us.

So plant a flower, a forget-me-not,
Carry me in your heart.
Remember now...forget me not.

Butterfly pretty
Butterfly a sign of love
Peace be upon you

CHASING A BUTTERFLY

Nine years old and chasing a butterfly,
Yet chasing away the boy with a net,
Loving the colours, alive and free!
Nine years old and *living*...because is why!

Twelve years old and chasing a butterfly,
Catching a Monarch with utmost of care,
Catching it gently straight out of the air,
Then lovingly setting it free, bye-bye.

Eighteen years old and getting a tattoo,
With a big butterfly pattern, of course,
A butterfly dancing a flight on the wing,
It makes the heart soar and the spirit sing.

Twenty-six years old and watching her child
Running across the lawn, light as the wind,
Chasing a butterfly, laughing with glee;
So sweet is the memory it makes her cry.

Years older now and the same scene repeats:
Now a grandmother and watching grandchild
Chasing a butterfly, snatching at joy,
Her hand reaches out, with hers, and they smile.

Older still now and some frailty sets in,
Memories now fade, and abilities stray...
But she tries her best and chases her thoughts,
Fighting some fights that she feels she must win.

Eighty-nine years old and wheeling away
In a chair in a home, plainly alone,
In her own little world, but still chasing,
Chasing that butterfly...because is why!

Nine years old and chasing a butterfly;
Running free across a field of green grass;
She's captured its beauty inside her soul...
Nine years old and chasing a butterfly.

———————————

Flower pretty, flower stands
Teardrop fall on stem
Pretty flower understands

I'M FINE

"I'm fine," she said, when the doctor asked,
As in the glow of certainty she basked.
The doctor looked at me. I shook my head.
Her power of reason must be dead.

Back home, she writhed in obvious pain.
She spurned my help in complete disdain.
To the paramedics she said, "No time
To be ill, don't you count me out, I'm fine!"

I took her back to that medical man;
She accused me of not even giving a damn.
He examined and prodded and asked me in mime—
She snapped with a snarl and told him, "I'm fine!"

When stricken at last and fatally ill,
The hospital doctors all took her in,
And though she faded, her spirit did shine,
And with her last breath she whispered, "I'm fine!"

We held a service to honour that gal,
Everyone came, every single last pal.
We toasted that feisty old gal o' mine,
By quoting her words from her will, "I'm fine!"

Then we gathered around for one last gin.
We confined her body though her spirit would win.
And we laid her to rest in a box of pine,
And wrote on her tombstone, Goodbye, "I'm fine!"

V. How We Remember Her

About the Author

H. W. Bryce came to poetry in a serious way when his wife was stricken with Alzheimer's disease. It was his way to deal with the anguish and depression that strikes most family care givers. Since then he has run the gamut of care giving experiences, and wishes to share his newfound insights.

Born in Saskatchewan, he has worked and lived in Ontario, where he earned his BA in English and Journalism; Alberta, where he continued his journalistic experience as a weekly newspaper editor-reporter-photographer, et al; and in British Columbia, where he worked as a book editor.

Mr. Bryce travelled extensively through Portugal and Spain, North Africa, and the Middle East in the 1960s, before settling in England. There, he met the lady who became his wife. They had one child together in London, where he worked as a teacher.

Later, in Worthing, Sussex, Mr. Bryce worked as a reporter with the Worthing Gazette and Herald. There, their second child was born.

When the world economy struck England, he moved his family to Hamilton, Ont., where their third child was born while Mr. Bryce worked at the Hamilton Spectator.

Today he lives and writes in Maple Ridge, BC.

CPSIA information can be obtained
at www.ICGtesting.com
Printed in the USA
LVOW11s1126260117
522214LV00005B/6/P